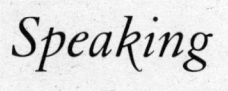

Speaking Out on Health

An Anthology

NEW WRITERS' VOICES
SIGNAL HILL

Speaking Out on Health

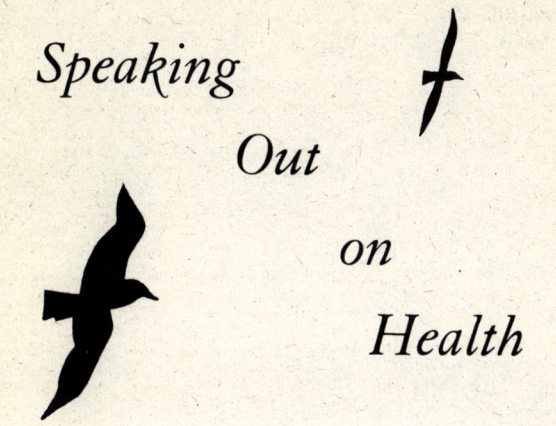

An Anthology

ATTENTION READERS: We would like to hear what you think about our books. Please send your comments or suggestions to:

Signal Hill Publications
P.O. Box 131
Syracuse, NY 13210-0131

• • •

SIGNAL HILL

Copyright © 1989 Signal Hill Publications
A publishing imprint of Laubach Literacy International

All rights reserved
Printed in the United States of America

10   9   8   7   6   5   4   3   2

ISBN 0-929631-05-6

First printing: January 1989

The words "New Writers' Voices" are a trademark of Signal Hill Publications.

Designed by Paul Davis Studio

The articles in this book were edited with
the cooperation and consent of the authors.

PRINTED WITH SOY INK

This book was printed on 100% recycled paper which contains 50% post-consumer waste.

Acknowledgments

We gratefully acknowledge the generous support of the following foundations which made the publication of WRITERS' VOICES and NEW WRITERS' VOICES possible: The Booth Ferris Foundation; The Vincent Astor Foundation; and The Scripps Howard Foundation. We also wish to thank Hildy Simmons, Linda L. Gillies, and David Hendin for their assistance.

We deeply appreciate the contributions of the following suppliers: Cam Steel Die Rule Works Inc. (steel cutting die for display); Domtar Industries, Inc. (text stock); Federal Paper Board Company, Inc. and Milton Paper Company Inc. (cover stock); Jackson Typesetting (text typesetting); Lancer Graphic Industries Inc. (cover printing); Martin/Friess Communications (display header); Mergenthaler Container (corrugated display); Offset Paperback Mfrs., Inc., A Bertelsmann Company (text printing and binding); and Stevenson Photo Color Company (cover color separations).

Our thanks to Paul Davis Studio and Claudia Bruno, José Conde, Myrna Davis, Paul Davis, and Jeanine Esposito, for the inspired designs of the books and their covers.

For their hard work and enthusiastic participation, we are most grateful to our student authors. We would also like to thank all the students who submitted articles for this book; although we were not able to include every piece, they were all good.

Contents

Dear Reader *1*

My Year of Terror
    Naresa Foster *6*

Sickle Cell Anemia and Me
    Forrestine Bragg *10*

Arthritis
    Emily Wall *16*

A Bad Experience with Tuberculosis
    Calvin Miles *18*

My Aching Back
    A Student *25*

My Arthritis
    Odessa Overby *29*

My Alcoholic Friend
    Nick Orlando *30*

My Accident Happened at the Factory
    Angel Tirado *31*

Me and the Special Olympics
  Tony Phillips 35

My Struggle for Independence
  Antonio Slaughter 40

Open Heart Surgery
  Ricardo Orengo 41

I'm Not Sick, I'm Just Down for Now
  Pearlie Walters 45

How I Dealt with Depression
  Fran DeBlasio 47

For More Information 51

WARNING

In this book, students tell about medical problems they have experienced. If, when you read about their symptoms, you feel that you may have the same problem—DO NOT try to treat these symptoms yourself. Instead, go to a doctor for advice. Similar symptoms can often have very different causes.

Dear Reader,

In early 1986, a group of students, tutors, staff members, and board members of Literacy Volunteers of New York City got together to talk about what we could do to get more good reading materials for our program. Someone said, "Why don't we do our own books?" And someone else said, "Why don't we do books written by students?" We decided to give it a try and called ourselves the Tutor/Student Publishing Committee of LVNYC.

The next question was, "What should the first book be about?" To find out, we sent a questionnaire to every student in the program. In their responses to the questionnaire, students listed their favorite kinds of books. When we reviewed all the questionnaires, we found that students liked books containing everyday experiences that people could relate to their own lives.

In the questionnaire, we also had a

NEW WRITERS' VOICES

list of subjects such as sports, religion, health, cooking, etc. We asked students to choose among all the subjects and tell us which were the most interesting to them. When we reviewed every student's list, we had about six subjects in which there was the most interest.

At that time, 16 students, representing eight tutorial sites, had been elected to the newly formed Student Committee of LVNYC. This was the first time that new readers from LVNYC's program had met to discuss issues of concern to literacy students.

The list was given to this committee, and they were asked to pick one subject for the first book. The committee decided that students were most interested in health—their own and others. It seemed that everybody would like true stories about health and illness. The committee also said they would help get students interested in writing articles for the book.

The Tutor/Student Publishing Com-

SPEAKING OUT ON HEALTH

mittee was happy with the subject. We also thought that new readers would want to hear about how people like themselves coped with health problems—not doctors or health professionals—just everyday people telling their own stories.

This is how the idea for *Speaking Out On Health* was born.

• • •

Over the next 18 months, we got many good manuscripts. From these we chose 13 pieces. They were then edited for publication.

We wanted to create a book that would cover a wide variety of health problems, so that many people could relate to it. *Speaking Out On Health* includes stories of how people faced such health problems as tuberculosis, arthritis, sickle cell anemia, cancer, and heart disease. It also includes stories about emotional problems and coping with death.

While each piece of writing is different, because each writer speaks in his or her own voice, all of the stories have three things in common:

One, all the writers decided to face their problems. They did not run away from them. They did not wait until it was too late. When they decided to face their problems, they found out how to ask for help—and how to get help.

Two, all the writers asked questions about their illnesses. They wanted to know what was happening to their bodies and their lives, so they learned how to get information from doctors, nurses, and other health care workers. They also talked with friends and read books about their condition. Most got more than one person's opinion on the subject.

Three, the writers are people who did not give up. They had faith in themselves. They just kept going.

SPEAKING OUT ON HEALTH

• • •

We hope that *Speaking Out On Health* makes you think about your health and your family's health. We hope it will encourage you to look for help if you need it or to ask for more information if you do not understand what someone tells you.

We also hope that reading this book inspires you to share your health concerns with others. If you write a story about a health problem, please send it to our editors. We will consider it for possible future publication. We don't want *Speaking Out On Health* to be our only health book!

—Forrestine Bragg, Melinda Corey, Fran DeBlasio, Calvin Miles, and Emily Wall, for the Tutor/Student Publishing Committee, Literacy Volunteers of New York City

My Year of Terror
Naresa Foster

This is the story of my year of terror over my health. It was the fall of 1973 when I first fainted. I was at work when my stomach started to feel funny. I made a cup of tea but it didn't help. I started to throw up and then I fainted.

My boss called the police and the police called an ambulance. They took me to the hospital. I stayed overnight. In the hospital, they just tested my blood and sent me away with a letter saying I was in good health. At that time I wasn't afraid. I thought I had fainted because of my bad eating habits. But when I fainted again, I began to get scared.

After the second attack, the doctor took x-rays and gave me another blood test. He still didn't find anything wrong with me. I got very frightened because I didn't know what was going on. I wondered if it was cancer and the doctors couldn't find it.

SPEAKING OUT ON HEALTH

A few months later, after my fifth attack, I went back to the hospital. I was there for eight days of tests and x-rays. They still found nothing.

A week later, I had still another attack. I worried about what would happen to my children if I had another long stay in the hospital for more tests. And what if they found it was cancer? Then I would have to be in the hospital for a long time.

I have an aunt who lives in Canada. I called her and asked her if she could come be with my children if I had to stay in the hospital. She said she could come. My daughters were twelve and ten at the time. They were good children. My heart felt better knowing my aunt could come.

Now that I had that settled, I went back to the doctor. He decided I needed more x-rays. He said, "If I can't find out what's wrong, we're in big trouble."

After he looked at the new x-ray, he said, "See, here is the problem. You have

NEW WRITERS' VOICES

gallstones. You will need surgery. Come in on Sunday morning and we will operate at 8 o'clock Monday morning." I went home and called my aunt. She came on Sunday and I went into the hospital.

On Sunday night, the nurse prepared me for surgery. On Monday morning, she gave me a shot to knock me out. A man came to take me to surgery. He said, "You aren't asleep." The doctor told him to give me another shot and put me on the table. The doctor said, "Now count from 1 to 100 backwards." I remember getting to 50.

I was scheduled to go home the next Thursday. On Tuesday, I found out I had pneumonia. The doctor called for a lung machine. When I coughed, I brought up a lot of blood. After three days, they took me off the machine and removed the IV tubes. They let me have some rice and soup. Four days later, I went home.

My children were very good while I

SPEAKING OUT ON HEALTH

was in the hospital. My older daughter came to visit me every day after school. The younger one couldn't come but she called me every night. They were both happy to have my aunt with them.

My employer and her children came to visit me and she called me every day. I had worked for the same people for nine and one-half years. After three months of rest, I went back to work. By now it was fall again, one year after my first attack.

In the year that I was sick, I was scared stiff. It was like the feeling a child has when she is stuck in a dark room and can't find her way out. Going back and forth to the doctor makes you afraid when you don't know what is going on inside of you. Once I knew what the problem was, I got it taken care of. The pain was hard on my inside, but I coped.

When I read this story that I wrote, I started to cry. I just couldn't help it. To remember the pain and the terror....

Sickle Cell Anemia And Me
Forrestine Bragg

Forrestine was seven when she had her first attack of sickle cell anemia at school. She was in her first grade classroom. The teacher had asked, "Can anyone tell me how to spell the word 'want'?"

"Ooh, ooh, me, I can spell the word 'want'!" Looking around the classroom to see if anyone else had their hand up, Forrestine wiggled out of her seat. "Ooh, me, I can spell that word," she said.

As Forrestine stood to spell the word, the teacher asked, "Are you all right? You don't look okay." "I'm fine," Forrestine replied. "Maybe you should see a nurse," the teacher suggested. Forrestine was sent home with a fever.

When Forrestine arrived home, her mother asked, "Are you having one of your attacks?" "Just a little pain in my arm and legs," she said. Her mother replied, "You should go to bed and get

SPEAKING OUT ON HEALTH

some rest." In a very sad voice, Forrestine asked if she could play with her younger brother Tyrone. "No, go to bed now," her mother insisted. Poking her lip out, Forrestine trotted off to bed.

At three a.m., Forrestine woke everyone with her crying and screaming. Forrestine's mother found her burning with a fever of 106°. Her hands and feet were swollen like balloons.

The next morning Forrestine went to her family doctor, Dr. Patrick. After he examined her, Dr. Patrick began to explain her condition to her mother. "Sickle cell anemia is a blood disorder that Forrestine has inherited," he said. "You and your husband are the carriers." While the doctor was explaining why Forrestine was in so much pain, Forrestine started screaming, "Mommy, my knee feels like a toothache."

The doctor continued, "A normal blood cell is round like a doughnut. Sickle cell blood cells are shaped like a banana. Forrestine now has bone damage to her knee, and she will have to walk with crutches for a while. She also has a touch of pneumonia. She needs to be hospitalized immediately."

In the hospital, Dr. Patrick explained more to Forrestine's mother about the illness. "Sickle cells make it difficult for oxygen to flow through the blood stream," he said. "It causes awful pain. It can cause other complications, too. For example, leg ulcers, pneumonia, strokes, and gallstones. Another symptom is jaundice. Forrestine's eyes and skin may turn pale or yellow."

Forrestine was discharged from the hospital and went back to school. As time passed, Forrestine spent more time in the hospital than in school. This was very frightening.

Later that winter on a cold Saturday morning, Tyrone called for his sister, "Get up! Get up! We are going shopping!" It was just seven more days until Christmas. Tyrone and Forrestine loved going shopping at this time of year. It

SPEAKING OUT ON HEALTH

was so special. You would see beautiful decorations, sidewalk Santas and sometimes the streets were covered in a white blanket of snow.

As they were going through the revolving doors at the store, Tyrone noticed that Forrestine looked sick. "Do you hurt?" he asked. "Just a little," Forrestine answered. "Please don't say anything to Mommy. She will take us home. Let's just have a good time shopping. And besides, you have a birthday coming up. I don't want to spend the holidays in the hospital."

Two seconds later, Forrestine had passed out. When she came to, she cried out, "Mommy, Mommy! Where am I? Why are these strange people with the long white coats standing over me?" "You're in the hospital," Forrestine's mother said.

As Forrestine tried to get out of bed, her right leg and arm lost their feeling. "I can't feel them!" she cried. "What is wrong with them?" "I don't know," said her mother. "That's why you have to stay here a couple of days."

The doctor told Forrestine's mother that Forrestine had had a stroke and that she needed to be in the hospital for at least a week or two, or maybe a month. During her stay in the hospital, Forrestine was scheduled for a lot of tests. She would see the doctor every day, sometimes twice a day.

One day when Forrestine's mother came to visit her, she heard the doctor tell her mother that most patients with sickle cell disease don't live past the age of 18. This was a very frightening thing to live with.

• • •

Today Forrestine is working very hard on building a career as an assistant coordinator in a literacy program. Having an illness that keeps her constantly sick is very difficult. When she gets sick, she gets treated for her illness. She picks up

SPEAKING OUT ON HEALTH

the pieces and continues with her life. The best she can do to handle her disease is to have a lot of faith in God. God will guide her. She is now 34 years old. Guess you could say that good things have finally begun happening to her.

Arthritis
Emily Wall

When I was 45 years old, I had to go to a hospital to have an operation. I had to stay there for two weeks.

While I was in the hospital, my legs started to hurt. I asked the doctor for some rubbing alcohol for them. The pain eased a bit. I told my friend, "I have been laying down so long, my legs hurt."

After I left the hospital, I went back to work. I was walking down the street and my legs gave way. My knees were hurting me so badly and were so hot to touch, I could hardly walk.

I tried everything for the pain. Nothing helped. I went back to Dr. Fried to find out why my knees were hurting me. Dr. Fried took an x-ray of my knees and told me to come back in a week. He would be able to tell me more then.

When I came back, Dr. Fried said, "You have arthritis." I asked the doctor, "What is arthritis anyway?" He told me

SPEAKING OUT ON HEALTH

that arthritis is aching in your joints with a lot of pain. Your joints get big. Years ago, doctors thought it was part of growing old. Now they aren't sure because even little babies can get arthritis.

The most important thing you can do for your arthritis is to follow your doctor's advice. You take your medication. And you don't give up if you are in pain. When you are on the go, it helps your joints. When you exercise, it makes you feel better. And I walk with my head held high so that oxygen can fill my lungs. I eat the right foods and get lots of rest.

Now I can dance again.

A Bad Experience with Tuberculosis
Calvin Miles

The first symptom of TB that I developed was a bad sweat. I thought it was the heat in the room. Then I developed a cough. I thought it was the cigarettes I smoked. The most dangerous symptom I had was a loss of appetite. In one year, I lost seventy pounds. I wouldn't go to the doctor.

The pain first hit me when I was at a friend's party. It ran through my chest like a bolt of lightning. I started to leave. My friend said, "Calvin, why are you leaving?" "I can't breathe," I told him. And I left the party.

As I walked toward the bus stop, I couldn't go a block without getting tired. When I got home, I took two aspirins. The next morning, I felt a little better. I knew I had to see the doctor.

The doctor examined me and said,

SPEAKING OUT ON HEALTH

"Calvin, you have to go to the clinic and have x-rays made." The next morning I went back to the doctor. He looked at the x-rays and said, "Calvin, you have to go to the hospital."

I went to the hospital on a rainy Saturday afternoon. It took four hours before I was admitted to the hospital. I didn't care if it took four years.

A lady took me to the E Building where I would be living for the next week. We got on the elevator and went to the fifth floor. Four or five men were standing around playing cards. I was given a bed near an old man who looked like he was dying.

That Sunday morning was kind of lonely. I was thinking about my job. I was thinking about when I would be able to go back to work.

On Monday morning, I went to the third floor. When I first saw her, I thought she was a nurse. She said, "Mr. Miles, I'm your doctor." My eyes lit up. I said to myself, a woman doctor! She said, "Mr. Miles, you have to take off your clothes." I said, "Why?" She said, "If you want me to examine you, you have to take off your clothes, Mr. Miles." I said no. I had never had a lady doctor examine me before. She was a beautiful woman. I think I fell in love with her.

Two days later, she came back to talk to me about the examination. She said, "Mr. Miles, I have some good news and some bad news." She had the tests back. "They are showing an infection. You have tuberculosis. But the good news is we think that we can cure you with several months of treatment." I said, "How long am I going to be in the hospital, Doctor?" She said, "Three months at the most." I felt good about that. I said to myself, it's not long. I had thought it would take longer.

I stayed on the fifth floor for two months. Then I was moved down to the fourth floor. That's when I saw the doctor again. She said, "Forget about three

SPEAKING OUT ON HEALTH

months. You will be here for about one year."

Finally, I couldn't take it any longer. I went to the nurse's office. I told her that I wanted to be discharged. She said, "Calvin, you know I can't do that. You have to see your doctor."

The next morning, I waited for the doctor to come in. When I saw her, I walked straight up to her and said, "Doctor, I have been in the hospital almost a year now. I want to be discharged. I can take care of myself now." She said no. She said, "Calvin, you know I can't discharge you because you have had only two negative sputum tests back."

I knew one patient who had had problems with his doctor. When he couldn't take it anymore, he jumped out the window. So I thought that if I could get the nurse to think I was going to jump out the window, maybe they would discharge me. Every morning after breakfast, I would go and stand by the window like I was going to jump out. I saw one of the nurses looking at me. One day, as I was going to look out the window, the nurse stopped me and said, "Calvin, are you all right?" I said, "No, I'm not all right. I want to be discharged." She said, "I can't discharge you."

Two weeks later, my doctor called me into her office. She said, "Calvin, you have been a good patient. I'm going to discharge you. But you have to promise me you will come back to the clinic three times a week." I can't tell you how I felt when she said that. I said, "Doctor, I don't care if I have to come back five times a week." On October 18, 1968, I was discharged from the hospital.

When I had been out of the hospital for about two weeks, I started thinking about the ways I could take care of myself. One of the things I did was stop smoking. Not being able to read, it was very hard to find out about tuberculosis. So I watched a lot of television to find out about it. I listened very carefully to what was said about the disease.

SPEAKING OUT ON HEALTH

I thought it would be good to exercise. When I went to the clinic, I asked the doctor what she thought about it. She said as long as I didn't overdo it, it was all right with her. I said to myself, I might as well start doing it right now. So I walked home. It was about five miles.

I knew walking was good for my legs, but I needed something to build up my lungs. I went back to the clinic and asked the doctor if it was all right to do some push-ups. She told me it was good to do them. Having this kind of disease, it was important to check with the doctor first. I started doing push-ups the next morning. The first time I did them, I felt like my lungs were going to collapse.

I went back to the clinic and told the doctor, "I better stop doing the exercises because my chest is hurting." She smiled and said, "Calvin, how long has it been since you exercised?" I said, "About a year." She said, "I wouldn't recommend this for every patient but you should go

NEW WRITERS' VOICES

back and continue your push-ups." Since then I've been doing push-ups every day for years.

• • •

Now I have read books about tuberculosis. I know more about the disease. I'm not afraid of it like I used to be. I turned a bad experience into a good experience.

My Aching Back
A Student

When I was 12 years old, I delivered groceries. Many customers would ask me to wash their windows in exchange for soda bottles. I would return the bottles to the store for money and give my mom half.

As I grew up, window washing was always there to fall back on ... and I did. Because of my reading problem, I had to work three times harder than those without one. A reading problem is hard to get around. But, with window washing, once you get to your job, all you have to do is wash windows—eight hours, ten hours, twelve hours a day.

Then I got into debt. I overdid my work—I washed windows until I got out of debt. I worked so hard that, one morning, I could not get out of bed.

The night before, while I was getting dressed to go out for dinner, I had a sharp pain on the right side of my face.

I ignored it, but the next morning, when I woke up, I could not get out of bed. I woke my wife up to help me. I realized that my back had given out.

My wife called a taxi and we went to the hospital. I thought that the doctor would give me some pills and I would be all right. In the emergency room, the doctor checked me over and said I had to be admitted. I had a slipped disk. He needed to take tests.

After the tests, the doctor said that I had to have an operation on my spine. I said OK, because I could not walk without the operation.

The doctor told me that I would have to find another type of work. I was scared. What could I do where I did not have to use my back and I did not have to read. I said to myself, I am in one of the biggest cities in the world. There must be something I can do but, first, I must get out of this hospital.

After the operation, I could not move. I was in pain. It felt like I had been hit

SPEAKING OUT ON HEALTH

by a truck. I hoped the pain would go away. I felt very helpless. I had to be fed. I had to be washed.

I wished I could sleep and not be disturbed, but they had to wake me for meals and exercise. Food was fuel. I knew I needed it. They told me I had to exercise. It was painful to move, but it had to be done. There was so much pain that I passed out many times. I worried about what I was going to do for a living. It was me and all my problems every day and every night.

I was in the hospital for four days. It seemed like four months! Then I was glad to be back in my own room with my own television. My wife and sister-in-law took good care of me. They made sure I ate before they went to work.

As time went by, I started to get around. I was bored staying in bed so I cleaned the house to keep busy. I started with the dishes. I couldn't believe it was such a big job for me. I had to balance myself by putting my elbows on the kitchen sink frame. It was hard, but I was proud to help with something.

A week later, I started to clean the stove. I couldn't complete the job. I left it for the next day. As I began to work, I began to enjoy my meals again. The more I worked, the better my meals tasted. I was putting on weight so my doctor told me to walk for exercise. I love to walk so I followed his advice. And that got me back into life.

I cleaned the floors and the walls and, finally, the windows. I painted the kitchen, the living room, and the bathroom. By then, I felt well enough to try cleaning some store windows. And before I knew it, I was working again. I was glad to go back to work because it was so rewarding. Self-pride!

My Arthritis
Odessa Overby

Some years ago, I was in the hospital because of my arthritis. Then I went back to work. A year later, I just had to stop work. I could not put in the time. I was in so much pain that I went back into the hospital. Because of my arthritis, I had to walk with a cane for two years.

I am not handicapped. I can do things for myself. I can do more and more every day. I have gone back to sewing in my home. I make dresses, suits, and pants for senior citizens. I mend and darn for people that I know. I sew and give fashion shows for my church. Between now and the twelfth of next month, my church needs 15 white dresses. I don't know what to do about it.

It is not hard to get better. I exercise and then I take a warm, not a hot, bath. If I sit too long, like when I am on the bus, I stand myself up. I wear warm clothing. I follow my doctor's orders. I don't give in to pain.

My Alcoholic Friend
Nick Orlando

My friend, John Smith, was an alcoholic. He couldn't hold a job because of his drinking. He would go out with his friends and they would drink a lot and have a good time.

John wanted to stop drinking because he was hurting his family. One time, he wanted to kill his wife and three kids. He realized then that he needed help. His friends told him about this group, Alcoholics Anonymous (AA). He started to go to meetings with some friends who belonged to AA. He was making good progress by going to the meetings.

He looked for a job and found one as a mechanic at a gas station. He was happy to get this job and he was doing well on the job. After six months, he got a raise. His wife and kids were happy for him. And he was happy also that he had stopped drinking. His life was back to normal.

My Accident Happened at the Factory

Angel Tirado

Some years ago I went to work at a nylon factory. We worked on machines cutting material. I cut samples from the material. We stretched them out on a frame and cut them square.

One day, I was switched to a machine that took water out of the material. The material came off rollers. I wore gloves to pull it out and put it in a barrel.

When I got there, the machine picked up speed and started going fast. It should have been running at a slower speed, so I went to shut the machine off. When I tried to do this, my gloves ripped and I got burned by the hot water. My hands were wet when I tried to shut the switch off and it started sparking. It scared me.

I must have jumped because, suddenly, I caught my finger in the machine's motor, which was next to the switch. I pulled my finger out. It really hurt. When

I saw my skin all cut up and the bone showing, I fainted. I think the foreman called the boss and he called the ambulance. They took me to the hospital.

At the hospital, they gave me surgery and medication and asked me questions. They called my family. I stayed in the hospital for two days and one night. My two brothers and my sister visited me and then took me home in a taxi. The hospital sent me to private doctors and they gave me exercises for my finger.

I was out of work for a month and a half. I was resting my finger and going to doctors. At that time, I was living with my mother. I didn't have to worry about paying the bills because she took care of me. I got $180 a week in disability payments.

I missed working. I wanted to go back to work, but at a different place. My uncle got me a job at a lamp factory.

A guy I knew at the factory gave me the name of a lawyer and I went to talk to him. He asked me a lot of questions.

SPEAKING OUT ON HEALTH

I told him what had happened. He told me I had to sue the company because they didn't have any insurance. I was angry at the company because they knew the machine was broken. So I decided to sue them.

There are special courts where you can sue companies that don't have insurance. I had to go to court a couple of times and to private doctors to get a report for the judge. He wanted to know if my finger was going to get any better and when I could start work again. I told the judge that the company knew the machine was broken. A friend that I worked with had told the foreman that the machine was broken.

In court, the judge found that the factory boss was lying. He made them pay me $5,000. I had to pay the lawyer out of that. I think he ripped me off and charged me too much. It was my first time and I didn't know much.

Now if I don't know how to use a machine, I ask someone who knows how to teach me. I'm not scared of machines anymore, because I make sure I know how to use the machine before I start.

I've also learned that you have to find out if the company you work for has insurance. I know my rights now.

Me and the Special Olympics
Tony Phillips

I was born in New York City in 1957. I've had cerebral palsy since birth. As a baby, I was completely bedridden because of my weak arms and legs. It seemed like I would be in bed for the rest of my life. My mother and father used to say that I would always have to live at home with them because of my disability.

From the ages of three to seven, I was in the hospital because I could get therapy there five days a week. I got to go home on weekends, except when I was recovering from an operation. By the time I was 12 years old, I had had 17 operations.

I cried a lot when I could not go home on weekends. It was very hard for me to be in bed all the time when I was little. I wanted to go out and play like other kids, but I just couldn't.

When I was 17, I started going to

NEW WRITERS' VOICES

United Cerebral Palsy (UCP). I've been going there ever since. My only experience with exercise before UCP was my therapy in the hospital. Those exercises were boring.

At UCP, I learned about the Special Olympics. There are about eight different classes of events in the Special Olympics. The class you are in depends on what parts of your body you use best. People who race using walkers are in Class 5. I started out in that class because I have to use a walker. Almost everyone in Class 5 has a very strong upper body.

Part of my disability is that I have trouble controlling my arms. Although I get around OK with a walker, I fall down if I go really fast and I have trouble staying in my racing lane.

One time, I was coming in last in a walker race. I got so mad, I threw the walker away and tried to finish on my own legs. I was so determined to do well that it felt like someone was pull-

SPEAKING OUT ON HEALTH

ing me to the finish line. I still came in last but I felt good about it because I had done the best I could. A coach noticed me in that race. He started to spend a lot of time working with me because he liked my determination.

My coach designed a special wheelchair for me to race in. He made it so I could push the wheels with my legs because they are stronger than my arms. But when you push the wheels of the chair, you go backwards and not forwards. So I race going backwards, looking over my shoulder to see where I am going. People who use wheelchairs every day are very good with them. Since I usually use a walker, I had to train very hard to get good at the wheelchair.

The Special Olympics are held from May to the end of September. I start to train at the end of January and stay in training until the season is over. Now I have two coaches, Bob and José. They made up a workout for me that I do twice a week when I'm in training.

Every season when I first start training, I feel sore. But soon the soreness goes away and I get more and more nervous and excited about the races coming up. Right now, I am not in training but I'm trying to stay fit so I won't have to do too much work when the season starts.

When we have the games, people come from all over the world to participate. The competition is good. You check out the opposition pretty carefully. I love to win but, even when I lose, I learn something from the person who beats me.

I used to defeat myself by being afraid. What is there to be afraid of? The worst thing that can happen if you lose is that you will decide racing is not for you. So you might as well try because otherwise you will never know.

On the day of the race, while we are sitting around waiting for our class to be called, I meet a lot of people. Anyone can be disabled—a doctor or a lawyer or a judge, and I can talk to them because we all have something in common.

Racing is the best thing I have ever done for myself. It has made me stronger physically so I get around better every day. I feel happier because I feel independent. I know I can take care of myself. My mother and father thought I would always have to live at home, and I proved that is not true. I used to feel depressed and sad sometimes. Now I just keep wondering, Who will I race against next year?

My Struggle for Independence
Antonio Slaughter

My name is Tony Slaughter. This story is about me. In case you didn't know, I have been disabled since birth. I have cerebral palsy. It's hard to move around. In the past, I didn't go out much. People were always saying I was lazy. I started to believe it, and this made me very depressed.

Then I learned how to take the bus. This was very important. A friend said, "You can do it. I will help you." In the spring when the weather was warm, my friend took me to all the bus stops in the neighborhood. He taught me how to get on the bus.

The first time I went on a bus alone, I was afraid. But, after a while, I was very glad to be with people. When I got home at the end of the day, I felt good inside.

Open Heart Surgery
Ricardo Orengo

It was 1965 and I was seven years old. I lived in Brooklyn with my family. I was a happy kid. But my parents were worried about me. Often my face would turn yellow and then purple. They would say, "Ricky, do you feel all right?" And I would say, "Yes, Pop and Mom." Finally my father said to my mother, "We must take Ricky to the hospital."

The next week I went to the hospital for a check-up. Afterwards, the doctor said, "Your son has a hole in his heart." My parents asked, "How did that happen?" "Maybe your son was born like that," the doctor replied.

"What can you do?"

"Your son needs an operation."

"What will happen if he doesn't get an operation?"

"Your son will die."

So my parents signed the papers for my operation.

The doctor told them I had to stay in the hospital and my parents took me to my room. The nurse said they had to leave. She said, "Your son will be safe." When my parents walked out the door, I started to run after them but two nurses stopped me. I started to cry.

I said to myself, Why did they leave me here? I was scared that I would not see them again. Then it was night. I couldn't fall asleep because I was worrying about my parents.

The next day the doctor came to see me. He said they would take me to the operating room. Two men put me on a stretcher. They took me to the operating room. They put me on the table. Someone put a mask over my face and said to count to ten.

I don't know how long the operation took. Then they put me in the recovery room. I opened my eyes very slowly and saw my parents. They asked me how I felt. "Very weak," I said.

When the doctor came to see me in

the recovery room, he asked me to move my arms and legs. "Good," he said. My arms and legs were all right. He said I could be moved back to my room.

When I got to my room, my parents were waiting. I was very happy to see them. I said to my parents, "I want to go home." But I stayed in the hospital for nine months.

On Halloween day, I was still in the hospital. Lots of kids have fun on Halloween. I went to the window. I saw kids trick or treating. I said, "I wish I had fun too, but I will get better."

Then it was Thanksgiving Day. Lots of kids have turkey. I had turkey in the hospital.

And then it was Christmas Day. Lots of kids get toys to play with. My parents came and brought me toys too. I was very happy to see them, but I wished I was home to see my brother. It is not fun in the hospital.

Finally, the doctor told me I would be going home soon. I was very happy.

The day I left the hospital was the best day of my life.

The years passed by. When I became a man, I got very sad. My mother asked me what was wrong. I said, "Mom, I hate my body. Lots of guys have husky bodies and I don't." She said, "Ricky, you are very lucky to be alive. We weren't sure you would live to see this day." When she said that, I was thankful.

I'm Not Sick, I'm Just Down for Now

Pearlie Walters

You should not take health for granted. When you get up in the morning and have no pain, you should thank God your body is in good shape.

I have been in and out of hospitals since 1971. I have had one operation after another for tumors. In 1980, I was in the hospital with endometriosis. Endometriosis prevents you from having children. Then I had an operation on my intestines and I have scar tissue.

I said to myself, Pearl, you know your problem. Now, you deal with it and make every moment count.

When I meet people who are sick, I tell them to be strong and not to feel sorry for themselves—and don't let others feel sorry for them either. When someone feels sorry for me, I tell them, "I'm not sick. I'm just down for now."

When your body is sick, you have to deal with it. But the rest of the time, I get out of the house as much as I can and keep myself looking good. I like to go out dancing, to the movies, and to dinner. I love people and being around them.

I don't have much time to think about my illness. You can kill yourself with self-pity. Sometimes, I tell my intestines, Hey, get it together in there. And I keep on going. I pray that my health problems will be solved.

How I Dealt with Depression
Fran DeBlasio

In the past, I didn't know how to deal with depression. When I lost my mother, I couldn't deal with the stress.

I saw my mother have a stroke right in front of me. I knew what was happening to her. My uncle called the ambulance. She went to the hospital. I was with her most of the night. She didn't know anything.

The next day, she opened her eyes and looked at my brother and me. I told her to fight. She couldn't talk to me but I said to her, "If you know what I am saying, just squeeze my hand." About ten minutes later, she opened her eyes again. Then she went into a coma for three weeks. I stayed by her side and did a lot of praying. I was so hurt. I didn't want to be with anyone. But I talked to my friend and did a lot of crying.

After my mother died, I lost a lot of

weight and couldn't work too well. I did not stop crying. The only way I could deal with my feelings was by talking with someone and crying with them.

After a year went by, I was still sad. My friends said, "Come on, let's go out." I said, "I don't feel like it." They said, "If you don't want to stay, you can go home." I said okay and went out with them. I didn't like going out. My best friend said, "I know what you are going through, but you have to start to do things." I said, "I know, but right now I just want to stay home."

My three close friends didn't give up. Where they went, they invited me along. If I hadn't had them to cry and talk with, I don't know what would have happened.

About two years later, my grandfather got sick. My aunt, uncle, brother, and I took my grandfather to the hospital for an operation.

When my grandfather came home from the hospital, he couldn't talk any-

SPEAKING OUT ON HEALTH

more. One day, my aunt asked me to get Grandfather up to eat. He wouldn't wake up so I called the ambulance. They came and took him back to the hospital. They said he had had a stroke. I knew he was dying. I felt so hopeless once again. I didn't know what to do.

Every day, I stayed with my grandfather in the hospital. I talked to him and I cried. Even though he didn't know me anymore, I told him I would be there until he died. I told him how much I loved him and how I knew he would be with my mother. I was the last one to see him alive.

After that, I was depressed for a long time. I saw my best friend and we talked. She said, "I know how hurt you are." I told her, "I want to die." She said, "At one time I wanted to die too. You need help." I said, "I know." She said, "Please go for help." When she started to cry, I knew that she was a good friend. She was worried about me. So I told her I would think about it.

The next day, I went to see a therapist and it has helped me. If it weren't for my three best friends, I wouldn't be here right now. I would have been lost if I didn't talk to my friends. I learned how to deal with things I could not change. I also learned not to blame myself when I try to help somebody and it fails. I went through a lot and dying is not the answer. You have to deal with your problems. If you can't deal with them by yourself, you should get help.

WARNING

In this book, students tell about medical problems they have experienced. If, when you read about their symptoms, you feel that you may have the same problem—DO NOT try to treat these symptoms yourself. Instead, go to a doctor for advice. Similar symptoms can often have very different causes.

For More Information

Here is a list of medical organizations that cover some of the diseases written about in this book. We have also added a few other organizations that could be helpful to you. You can write or call them for the information you need. You may also find local phone numbers for some of these associations in your telephone directory.

ALCOHOLISM

Alcoholics Anonymous
P.O. Box 459
Grand Central Station
New York, NY 10163
(212) 870-3400

Hazelden Foundation
Box 176
Center City, MN 55012
(612) 257-4010

National Council on Alcoholism
  and Drug Dependence
12 West 21 Street
New York, NY 10010
(212) 206-6770
(800) 622-2255

ARTHRITIS

Arthritis Foundation
1314 Spring Street, NW
Atlanta, GA 30309
(404) 872-7100

CEREBRAL PALSY

Wheelchair Sports USA
3595 E. Fountain Blvd.
Suite L-1
Colorado Springs, CO 80910
(719) 574-1150

United Cerebral Palsy Associations
1660 L Street NW
Suite 700
Washington, DC 20036
(202) 842-1266
(800) 872-5827

DEPRESSION

National Depressive and Manic
  Depressive Association
730 North Franklin
Suite 501
Chicago, IL 60610
(312) 642-0049

Foundation for Depression and
  Manic Depression
24 East 81 Street
New York, NY 10028
(212) 772-3400

ENDOMETRIOSIS

Endometriosis Association
8585 North 76th Place
Milwaukee, WI 53223
(414) 355-2200

GENERAL

National Black Women's Health Project
1237 Ralph David Abernathy Blvd. SW
Atlanta, GA 30310
(404) 758-9590

A national organization that sponsors educational programs and self-help groups on health issues important to black women.

HEART DISORDERS

American Heart Association
7272 Greenville Avenue
Dallas, TX 75231
(214) 373-6300
(800) AHA-USA1

National Heart, Lung and Blood Institute
PO Box 30105
Bethesda, MD 20824-0105
(301) 251-1222

HIGH BLOOD PRESSURE

National Hypertension Association
324 East 30 Street
New York, NY 10016
(212) 889-3557

SICKLE CELL ANEMIA

Sickle Cell Disease Foundation of
  Greater New York
127 West 127 Street
Room 421
New York, NY 10027

Sickle Cell Disease Association of America
200 Corporate Point
Suite 495
Culver City, CA 90230-7633
(310) 216-6363

TUBERCULOSIS

American Lung Association
1740 Broadway
New York, NY 10019
(212) 315-8700

Seven series of good books for all readers:

WRITERS' VOICES
Selections from the works of America's finest and most popular writers, along with background information, maps, and other supplementary materials. Authors include: Kareem Abdul-Jabbar • Maya Angelou • Bill Cosby • Alex Haley • Stephen King • Loretta Lynn • Larry McMurtry • Amy Tan • Anne Tyler • Abigail Van Buren • Alice Walker • Tom Wolfe, and many others.

NEW WRITERS' VOICES
Anthologies and individual narratives by adult learners. A wide range of topics includes home and family, prison life, and meeting challenges. Many titles contain photographs or illustrations.

OURWORLD
Selections from the works of well-known science writers, along with related articles and illustrations. Authors include David Attenborough and Carl Sagan.

FOR YOUR INFORMATION (FYI)
Clearly written and illustrated works on important self-help topics. Subjects include: Eating Right • Managing Stress • Getting Fit • About AIDS • Getting Good Health Care, among others.

TIMELESS TALES
Classic myths, legends, folk tales, and other stories from around the world, with special illustrations.

SPORTS
Fact-filled books on baseball, football, basketball, and boxing, with lots of action photos. With read-along tapes narrated by Phil Rizzuto, Frank Gifford, Dick Vitale, and Sean O'Grady.

SULLY GOMEZ MYSTERIES
Fast-paced detective series starring Sully Gomez and the streets of Los Angeles.

WRITE FOR OUR FREE COMPLETE CATALOG:

Signal Hill Publications
P.O. Box 131
Syracuse, NY 13210-0131